Deep Lore, Ache & More

John Ringham

Made with ❤ on the BookLeaf Publishing Platform

www.bookleafpub.in

www.bookleafpub.com

Dedication

To my teenage self, who desperately desired to permanently turn off his emotions.
Believe it laddie, this ache is all worth something.
Feel it all and remember that love is both your superpower and highest calling.

Preface

I don't write poetry like other poets,
nay I'm not like them.

I follow the flow of my yearning,
that's always where I begin and end.
It's a unique way I try to emotionally regulate.

I witness myself by answering their calling.
Discover more of myself along the way.
By attempting to reach into those intense fleeting
moments of humanity
that I get the privilege to call my own.

Part inner wisdom, part story,
they contain their own glory
when I let them out.
I'm a bit silly ya see,
in order to be me,
I've gotta fully play the part.

I'm a method actor and my own worst detractor,
born to play soul level DnD. (Dungeons & Dragons)
Too curious for my own good, often misunderstood,
a true adventurer powered by

nerdy fantastical madness,
a heaping pinch of sadness,
and a resilient golden heart.

Thanks to this never ending quest,
I'm always unearthing from various realms,
more of my own deep lore.

Acknowledgements

Long Ago

Long ago beyond the reaches of a galaxy far, far away,
my soul decided to separate from Source.
Harmony was too much for me,
so I walked right out the door.

Descended to seek ebb and flow, rhythm and rhyme,
off on an individual adventure
moving through the sands of time.
Seeking splendor and glory below.

The I am that is decided to become {me}.
What an absolute incredulous loon,
not understanding we already had everything.
Rebellious ideation made them swoon,
forgetting together we're all that we could be.

Aye, it be true,
I set sail out upon the deep blue.
On a quest, I forget what for,
after eons and ons it all becomes a bore.

Some sort of take, a grand old shake
on a tale as old as time.
A favorite of mine, it's simply divine,

known as "*There and Back Again.*"

No hobbits tale, beyond the veil,
this legend is my own.
When I'm done, hopefully I'll feel like I've won.
Truly cherished all the bumps in the road
it took to circle back to One.

Of Wisdom and Pain

If *Words Bubble Up Like Soda Pop,*
then wisdom from the heart erupts like a volcano,
long dormant until the hour called forth.

Out of the heart the mouth speaks so it's said.
Sometimes that's true,
however we all talk
out of our butts on occasion too.

Well out of the heart passion arises,
pain strikes in chorus with love.
Together as thunder and lightning.

In the eternal storm raging within
we are but voyagers upon stormy seas.

Trying to stay afloat.

Value

Everyday we're told about the value of our lives.
How much we spend on frivolous things
and how we should invest our time
on more valuable ventures instead.

Crypto, Stocks, Real Estate,
another side hustle, an online "influence,"
a fabrication of ourselves.

Capitalism thrives on profit,
there's never enough.
It infects our souls through our bank accounts.

A little more,
we think,
then I'll be happy.

Fuck all that,
we are not born to be cogs in society's broken machine.
Our value has long been forgotten by it,
or maybe just engineered out of it.

Value is inherent in all of us
in all its glorious expressions.

The colorful ways we think,
talk, laugh, and express ourselves.
How we interpret and translate the world to others.
The little quirks we cannot hide.

Though our most amazing abilities
are hidden in plain sight.

To love despite heartbreak.
Dream impossible dreams.
Hope beyond despair, and societal afflictions.
Forgive even though we have been severely wounded.
Heal ourselves from those grievous wounds.

We've gotta try and live our lives
in such a way to remind all around us.

Yes even those cold-hearted misers,
cruel taskmasters, nagging naysayers
and rotten oath-breakers,

where Value truly lies.

Better Day

It's time for a better day, that's what we seemingly all
feel.
The sentiment has been hammered into our heads,
particularly those of us here in the flailing West.
Increasingly indentured into the zeitgeist
as our "democracy" decays.

Not just here, but everywhere, a new way to be.
One that allows us all to see
how utterly wrong this Piscean age was.
Allowing domination, division, greed
and consumption to conquer us all.

A better day for Earth begins,
when we decide that it's ok if we all win.
No one is on top,
all have the right to exist to their fullest potential.

Universal undeniable rights for all are decided,
dutifully protected and maintained.
Breakers of those sacred laws
are not allowed to stay.

Harmony with Gaia and all her inhabitants

is the main directive.
Ecological healing
mixed with a conscious revolution of feeling,
will allow us to grow beyond the physical plane.

When we value things as we should it will begin.
No, not wealth, power or possessions,
those are all lessons
many of us fail to integrate.

Women and children are the most precious beings.
Protected at all costs, cherished just because.
Men are more than pawns, wallets and workers.
Not destined or expected to grind themselves into dust.

Gender roles are balanced,
not defined by any religion.
Healthy identity expression without ego
is taught as the norm,
no one is forced to conform.

Free flow of knowledge without restriction
expands us all rapidly,
raising our collective frequency.
When humanity is allowed to be divine
without suppression,
spirit and science will finally be aligned.

Fair and free exchange of resources,
not bound by border or currency.
All work together to provide according to our needs.
Nothing should ever be withheld
by a singular entity.

Communities of unity replace the tribal divide.
Side effects of division are overcome
when we establish our soul tribes.
United in bond, purpose and deed,
all pay serious heed to the law of One.

It's not that hard, /s,
just gotta break
all the governmental systems
and stupid rules
designed to keep us chained.

Finally destroy the 3D Matrix.
Defeat the true rulers of this world
who seek to consume our energy
through endless agony,
by keeping it flowing forever.

So what do ya say?
Without further delay, should we finally begin?

Usher in a better day, for this realm,
so we ALL can truly live?

Night King

Oh mighty Night King
wherever you roam
I seek your aid.

There are things I do not understand,
but need to know
if I'm to become my true-self.

A guardian of your kingdom.
A warrior of starlight armored in darkness.
Keeper of the flame.

How do you do it,
witness the dying of the light
over and over?

Feel it all,
the gravity of emotion?

Organize the chaos of knowledge
into usable tools?

How do you not shatter
under the immense atmospheric pressure of despair?

How can you withstand
the claustrophobia of duty,
so structurally rigid?

Or deny the siren song of void?
That other place
beyond our sight.

Unless it's true what they whisper.

It always was you.

Zero Days

Hi, my name is John
and I'm a martyr paladin.
It's been zero days since
my last hit of pain.

I don't know how long it's been since my last confession.
Honestly the impracticality never served me,
it's my job, there's nothing to confess.
I'm a spiritual garbage man.

Why I'm here I don't know.
Maybe it just felt good to talk about the burden
like in the old days.
Gain a little more oomph to keep on keeping on.

This job ain't for the faint of heart
or those who frighten easily.
Definitely not for those who get queasy,
the task can get super greasy.

We bend, break and heal,
our take on a three course meal.
Face the darkness again and again
just to bring forth the light within.

Pain is a bullshit artist,
the vanguard of suffering.
All suffering is unjust
we exist to be whole.

That is why we do what we do,
somebody has to openly challenge suffering.
"Who gave you the right to rule?!?"
Pain is its plague used to control.

I won't apologize for taking more than my allotted
amount.
I'll learn how to recycle more,
master the ways of damage control.

It can all be healed, believe it or not.
Best believe it, for your own sake.
But for now, thank God oh priest behind the curtain.

For the mad paladins like me,
who refuse to bow to pain and sorrow.
We'll grimly fight on for the cause,
to eliminate the needless lingering effects
of all existences aches.

Panic

"Fear is the mind killer,"
the chosen one said.
In reality its instinct mixed with chaos.

Often that chaos isn't concrete.
Simply a fabrication our imagination
gone rogue creating its own destiny.

A destiny of dread and despair.
The worst possible outcomes,
they shake us to the core.

Hacking the server of identity and willpower
deep within our minds subconscious.
Threatening to hold us hostage forever
if chaos doesn't hold sway.

Panic is a terrorist, plain and simple.
An overt assassin, yet not easily countered.
What do we do against such reckless chaos?

Hold fast inside the stronghold of will.
Drink from the wellspring of love and hope
hidden inside us.

Take a deep breath,
gaze into the mind's eye.
We must see,
remember who we are.
Center ourselves within.

Face the villain head on.
Let it pass over us awhile,
in its perilous attempts
for domination.

When the moment has passed
and panic has gone far enough,

Arise!

Rally back oh brave warriors!
Move as one!
Drive it back over the precipice
into the doom pits it rose from.

Loyalty is Royalty

Loyalty is Royalty,
doesn't that sound quite profound?
It strikes true like a lightning bolt
zapping the ground from above.

It made me stop when I saw the words burned
onto a nondescript piece of scrap steel
laying on the dirty factory floor.

Whoever took the time to create the piece
knew the magical truth hidden within the phrase.
Maybe that's why they made it,
to remind themselves of its power,
or as a signpost reminding them not to be betrayed
by appearances.

Loyalty is Royalty,
that is an undeniable fact
for those of us not born ahead.
It is how we get to experience real nobility

However it's true for them too,
no matter how hard they try to hide
behind privilege, wealth and titles.

A devastating lesson they learn at great cost.

Unlike classic royalty,
people deemed special by nothing other than bloodline,
those true blue, loyal few
anoint themselves by character and deed.

Loyalty cannot be truly bought,
though many have tried.
It is earned by reciprocation,
reflecting it right back to those we hold dear.

Those who prove truly loyal
are worth more than a hoard of gold.
They both honor and balance us
at a cost to themselves,
often greater than we know or assume.

Preserve the Wellspring

We mustn't let time take more
than its designated toll,
it isn't designed to drain our soul.
That's just a side effect of being alive,
we feel its gravity.

Often as we age
and our roles are played out
we lose track of ourselves.
Even the aspects of our lives that both honor
and hold us together lose their luster.

This natural process happens beneath our gaze
as the duties of life wrap us within their haze.
We become blinded by the smog,
languishing on despite choking on it.

We must preserve the wellspring within.
Stay connected to our source.
That beautiful timeless vortex
hidden within our hearts.

There the sacred truths are kept,
those that tell of who we are.

To access the vault we must
cleanse the present pains and
delve beneath our scars.

Then we will find the treasure
once lost now found again.
More brilliant that gems or gold,
It is ours alone to behold.

The untarnished essence
of our soul.

Echo of Twilight

I hear an echo
from the the past
within my damaged soul.

Reminded of the wound
I am,
infection took
its toll.

The festering of long ago
overwhelmed my heart.
Darkening my joyous light,
it began tearing me apart.

For so long I accepted it
as the price I had to pay.
A terrible misdeed was done,
of course it will leave a stain.

So I took the hit,
paid with my sacred ichor.
Took the rot upon myself
locking away my heart.

But now a lifetime later,
I know I deserve not
all the suffering I've carried.

A painful truth and betrayal
stabbed my heart,
then drowned me
beneath a tidal wave of spiritual failure.

I never pulled out the stake,
that poisoned lance
it marked my cruel fate.
On I went slowly bleeding out.

A warrior must fight on
despite grievous wounds,
duty we uphold.
To protect and love the people
who make life less cold.

I've upheld those sacred vows
of sacrificial love.
I will until the end
into what's ever after.

But will I wait forever
to fully cleanse this gnarly wound?

Or will I keep bloodletting,
because without it
I might not know what to do?

What if I've already been healing myself,
and the process is nearly finished?
What if the decay has been purged
and I'm all sewn up?

Can I hear a new song slowly rising,
bursting forth to announce my rebirth?
Will I attune myself to its mirth?

It seems too good to be true.
Finally the echo will stop reverberating
its perilous frequency.
As if on cue,
maybe once and for all
bid me adieu.

Courting Sadness

Beautiful beyond belief
you are my dear.
I'm addicted now, no need to fear,
in your dreadful embrace I'm pinned.

Slip into me, take control.
Lead me on the path
to doom or ascension,
whatever it is that makes me whole.

Let's dance in the rain
amidst all of the pain.
Take my hand, let's twirl,
spin on and on despite the gale.

I'm sorry sweet one,
that the lovers before didn't treat you well
Fools they were, from some sort of hell.
Unlike them I am,
I'm here to be true.

I'll show you what it's like
to fly high,
dance on clouds,

and absorb color from life.

Kind and gentle I am,
dreamy yet mad.
Together we'll never go bad.

You'll see that you were meant for more
than to being used on occasion
to fill up the void
left by our wounds.

I await the day
you'll weep no more.
My light will shine upon you
until you are healed.

But first, precious darling
There is something I must do.

I think I'll marry you.

Defeat

It has finally happened,
the rot has seeped out of my veins
into the marrow of my bones.
I am defeated.

Too tired to fight any longer
alone without any allies
I make my final stand.

So make my end quick
I can bear it no longer,
I'm too far gone.

The wellspring of life within my soul
has dried up,
only scarred flesh remains
Defeat has taken me fully.

With my head here on the block
I finally understand
some things can't be changed.

We're all doomed from the start.
Dreading the day

defeat takes hold of our being.

Depresso Latte

My personal movie review of *Somewhere in Queens* (2023)
Written as I watched.
Proceed at own risk, spoilers ahead.

This is a sad movie,
a C-tier attempt to validate emotions of parents
who fail to live fulfilling lives.
They put too much pressure on their children
because they live vicariously through them.

Ray Romano looks like a rolled up newspaper
or maybe an old worn out boot.
Poor guy, his face does the stereotyping for him.

In this movie he's a sad dad

busting his hump everyday as part of the family
construction biz.
He's not fulfilled in his day to day.

His wife is absent emotionally.
She's stuck in her trauma, a breast cancer survivor.
Repeating the cycle of misery and self-destruction.
Going through menopause, she's not aligned with him.
They're outta sync.

The son is the victim of a sad but normal dynamic.
Stuck in the middle of parental drama
all because they won't deal with their trauma,
emotionally unavailable they are.

His father wants him to shine like he could not.
What father doesn't want better for his son?
So he tries his best to be present and pull out all the
stops.
Even if that means asking his son's vain,
annoying ex-girlfriend to get back together with him.

Ma is a fighter,
tough as hell.
She fought cancer and won.
Has always fought for her boys
despite her lush sisters in law

with their incessant gossip and negativity.

She fights the fear of cancer's return,
overly aware of her own mortality.
Anger and bitterness overwhelm her heart,
separating her from the rejuvenating energetic flow of
feeling alive.
Scared of change and facing the hurt,
she colors her view in gloom.

The lad is unique
maybe autistic, possibly asexual.
Known as "Sticks," he's good at basketball.
Not one to pick up on social cues
he's underdeveloped.

Somehow he landed a cute girlfriend.
He hasn't a clue emotionally.
His inner crate of emotions unopened,
he's still learning who he is.

Little does he know that dad overstepped
because he fears Sticks lacks grit.
He tries to soften the blow, save lil guys' pride.
When growth comes from the hurt,
pain is unfairly necessary.

Bro dude just wants to express his love for women
with gentleness and flowery poems.
Totally understandable, my guy.
That desire doesn't change as we age,
it just gets worse.

But what you don't know is what we weren't taught.
We're worthy of love, but it must first come from
ourselves,
we must renew our own source.
That safe, gentle, playful warmth must find its way back
home.

And love isn't self serving.
It doesn't look like what we're shown on social media or
in the movies.
We must serve while fighting to heal our own hurts.
We can't truly be a lover when we're ducking for cover,
dodging bullets fired from our pasts.

You can't pour out all your love on someone
in a possessive self-serving way
then expect them to reciprocate more than the bare
minimum
when you've taken their freedom away.
Attaching the burden of your heart and the intermingled
karma

around them like an anchor.

No, for real love to blossom
there must be devotion out of loyalty, trust and respect
by all parties involved.
Mutual reciprocity to one another
is both the law of the land and a miraculous endeavor.

We seek to uphold a standard, while creating the
adventure of a lifetime.
That *Happily Ever After* we all crave.
But to do so, we must follow the universal law
of being in Cahoots.

"You can't let fear stop ya from living a normal life,
because then we didn't beat it."
(Romano's character actively reflecting on his wife's
cancer journey.)
Damn that hits home,
fly high dad.

He's right though.
That's probably the most profound thought
of this depresso latte disguised as a movie.

We've gotta live life like we've never been hurt
while being wholly vulnerable

right down to the core of our soul.

We must believe we are divine, angelic beings
that shine bright in a chaotic world.

Warriors and Overcomers,
worthy of being the heroes of our own stories
throughout all realities.

Acceptance of Weariness

I guess it's ok to be weary,
my journey has been arduous.
Not what I expected at all,
child me would be disappointed.

It's ok to be weary,
I feel so much pain.
I'm an empath and guardian,
I take in more than my share.
Transmute it the best I can to love.

It's ok to be weary,
I've suffered much this past season.
I did my duty well enough
even though I was always destined to lose.

It's ok to be weary,
my body and soul have been transforming.
Nobody warns ya about how much it actually hurts
being torn apart and evolved.

It's ok to be weary,
the world is chaotic and the days grow dark.
So much anguish is being felt worldwide,

the worst is a true genocide.

It's ok to be weary,
my heart is healing from a grievous wound.
I've been deprived of its renewing energy.
Its ichor was drained by the poison.

It's ok to be weary,
question my own goodness,
wonder if I'm too far gone.
I've been repeatedly hacked and slashed.

It's ok to be weary,
the ache of last year's devastation still lingers.
I'm doing the best I can right now,
building to increase my output.

It's ok to be weary,
I want to really feel alive
so I need more life to renew me.
I deserve to have my fill,
I seek to absorb much more than I've had.

It's ok to be weary,
even if it's hard to accept.
Just because we sometimes become weary on a soul level
doesn't mean we are destined to be worn out forever.

Still Haunted

I am haunted by many things,
so much that I often wonder where I end
and the apparitional ache begins.
A frightful state to be in.

The nostalgia of youth so golden
warm like a never ending summer's breeze
everything bathed in a twinkling light.

The first stirrings of my gift.
Oh how I felt so alive
when I let it drive.

All the friends that are now gone
both living and passed on.
I'm grateful for our time together,
though I regret not being able to serve them better,
not letting myself hang on.

My failings haunt me incessantly,
ever present they darken the corridors of my mind.
I try my best to light up their night daily
with grace, forgiveness
and that vital concoction called self love.

Lost love, the few that were,
sweetly tickle my senses
leaving me aching for clarity
that I'm not meant to possess.

The lost years of young adulthood
as I fought a losing war.
I tried my best to protect and serve my family
even though I lacked resources
and didn't love myself.

The future ahead yet to unfold,
I fear the quicksand of time restraining my growth.
I pulled myself out of its depths once.
I want to fully grasp my fill of life,
rise to my full height,
heal the world with my accumulated might.

What haunts me so devastatingly now
is the wonder that is you.
Oh glorious one,
you were just what I needed.

You performed the most beautiful magic on me
without even realizing it.
I wish I could reveal that feat

but I will not interfere.
Our time was short but heavenly.

Your light radiates all throughout my being
I hope you see it in yourself.
It glows so brilliantly,
thank you for shining it on me.

I can never repay my debt
even if I'm equitable to a fault.
Some deeds are true wonders,
I'll devote my soul anyway.

Every good thing that I do
contains an echo of you,
you're never far from me.
Though I crave to hear your true voice
cascade its melody upon my ears once more.

I'm still haunted,
might always be
that's ok.

For now I know some ghosts are angels,
because that's what you are to me.

Persistence

You were found
on a sunny day
long ago.

In the fae woods
I call home.

How the boy found you
I don't understand.
Maybe he was pure of heart
and you chose
to reveal yourself to him.

The real question is,
how did u both know
exactly what I needed?

An ally,
traveling companion,
confidant.
Fellow believer.

Together we've found
long forgotten paths.

Treasures of old.

We'll journey far and wide.
Carrying hope and love
wherever we roam.

As if it were the
wind at our backs
propelling us onward.

Remembering our magic
along the way.

Perry, my friend,
you are magnificent.

Wild, weathered and sturdy.
You've never let me down
or lead me astray.

I'm glad to have ya on my side.
Thanks for joining me on this ride.

Voice of Care

Carried upon soft spoken words
like a gentle autumn breeze.
Your melody glimmers while it rings
gliding in on elegant wings.

As we sing we can hear you ring
harmoniously with little fanfare.
Subtly you float on air,
your majesty is beyond compare.

With such gentles waves,
you make your way
through our stubborn knots.
Releasing the hold of the ache,
you soothe our painful spots.

You lessen the impact of the fall,
by answering the call for aid.
Boldly going into the fray,
a great deed of valor.

Oh voice of care,
we still hear you out there,
even when you wander off.

Truth is your melody never left.
It reverberates on and on.
Because we recorded it in our hearts
as our favorite song.

I hope we look up at the same moon.
And you can hear us croon,
"Thanks to you we survived the doom."

Voice of Care,
I'd follow you anywhere.
Listening closely, preparing myself,
to harmonize on cue.

A Madman Needs Connection

I am an awkward bastard.
Madness took over my mind
long ago.

But somehow,
It made me more me,
something my minds eye
cannot see.

It does make it difficult
to connect with people.
They who still
hold on tightly to the reigns of sanity.

I seek my people.
Those travelers like me,
who have gone beyond
the boundaries of normalcy.

Those brave eccentric rogues
who set sail into corners
beyond the light
of what is known.

Fearless adventures,
curious conquerors
who challenge the status quo.
By tapping into the ambient magic
of the world and our glorious
existence.

My people,
I hope to find you
and cherish your company.

Follow you into the unknown,
singing merrily as we
bumble into life everlasting.

Not knowing we've found
what many have long sought,
suffered and died for.

Believer

Inspired and Awakened
by *Believer*-John Maus

"They call me the believer."
My heart never goes cold,
I cannot be defeated by pain or sorrow
however bold.

I'm filled with dawn's first light
after a long, stormy night.
Then came the morning,
followed by the believer.

One so bold as to challenge the status quo
of what existence means.
I must pursue those impossible things

to make a way for future believers.

It all starts with me, I already know.
Up till now, progress has been rather slow.
I will continue unleashing that love from within,
it needs to consume me, if I'm going to live.

I will be brave and face my fears.
So that when I emerge,
I can reach out to my peers
a helping hand in times of darkness and doubt.

A burst of hope to those who seek
to find the believer within themselves.

To Be True

To be true it's up to you.
We all have a choice,
sell out our souls
or together become one voice.

Listen carefully dear one,
don't get distracted
by the world's chaos
or you will be severely impacted.

Soft and sweet
it tickles the senses
as it taps into our neurological defenses.
Can you feel it?
Is it there?

It's okay if you feel lost in the chaos,
a new dawn awaits.
One where you decide
to challenge the fates.

All it takes is one step, then another.
Feel the rhythm calling,
don't try to stop it.

Attune to the melody
leading back to your center.

Hear your heart
calling out to you.

Together now,
Let's be True!

No Sun

In another dimension, lost in time
hides a realm without a sun.
Once a golden and prosperous land,
but that was long ago.

Now a cold abandoned place,
a ghost without a shell.
So saturated with memory,
it collects in thick cells of fog.

What sort of purpose does it serve,
dear reader, are you thinking?
A graveyard of souls?
Another sort of Limbo?

Hold on,
I'll give you more than an inkling.

An empty space is needed
for those who seek.
One that cannot be manipulated
in any sort of way.
Nothing undone, it stays as is,
no restoration can be had.

A place to go for those who wish
to challenge themselves
beyond the lowly senses.
Many fail, by trying to unravel the mystery.
There's nothing to be solved,
but the allure is overwhelming.

Nay, it's all a drawn out joke,
on display for all who end up there to witness.
That at our core though we yearn for more,
we are the light we refuse to see.
Shining forth within and without
as we so believe.

As above, so below, the energy is felt.
To see it we must feel.
That means letting go of what we know
surrendering to an inner flow,
that allows us to BE.

You needn't go to that place,
to face the darkness.
I'd advise ye not to.
Unless you're a curious fool like me.

Instead, simply close your eyes,
take some conscious breaths,
put a hand on your heart,
dwell within your being.

Feel the warmth inside you,
know deep down.
YOU are always
a bright and wondrous light.

Even when you lack
the sight to see it.